rockschool®

POPULAR MUSIC THEORY

Workbook

GRADE 6

www.rockschool.co.uk

Acknowledgements

Published by Rockschool Ltd. © 2015
Catalogue Number RSK011509
ISBN: 978-1-908920-75-1

Publishing
Written, compiled and edited by Simon Troup, Jennie Troup and Stuart Slater.
Internal design and layout by Simon and Jennie Troup, Digital Music Art.
Cover designed by Philip Millard, Philip Millard Design.
Additional proofing by Chris Bird, Owen Bailey, Nik Preston, Mike Stylianou, Joanna Taman and Mary Keene.

Syllabus Consultants
Rachael Meech, Mike Stylianou, Joanna Taman and Anna Cook.

Contributors
Prof. Joe Bennett, Simon Niblock, Jonathan Preiss, Stefan Redtenbacher, Philip Henderson and Martin Hibbert.

Images & Illustrations
p. 22 | © iStock.com/craftvision
p. 24 | © Bruce MacQueen / Shutterstock.com
p. 26 | © Yarchyk / Shutterstock.com
p. 26 | © Anton Havelaar / Shutterstock.com
p. 26 | © yoshi0511 / Shutterstock.com
p. 30 | © Andrey_Popov / Shutterstock.com
p. 30 | © iStock.com/sappono
p. 31 | © Miguel Garcia Saavedra / Shutterstock.com
pp. 32 & 54 | © iStock.com/ayzek

Printing
Printed and bound in the United Kingdom by Caligraving Ltd.

Distribution
Exclusive Distributors: Music Sales Ltd.

Contacting Rockschool
www.rockschool.co.uk
Telephone: +44 (0)845 460 4747
Email: info@rockschool.co.uk

Table of Contents

Introductions & Information

Page

Theory Exam Sections

Page

Sample Paper

Page

Additional Information

Page

Welcome to Rockschool Popular Music Theory – Grade 6

Rockschool publish two sets of books to help candidates prepare for theory examinations – the *Rockschool Popular Music Theory Guidebooks* and *Rockschool Popular Music Theory Workbooks.*

The guidebooks are a teaching resource for candidates to work through the material required for the Rockschool theory syllabus with the support of their teacher.

To complement the guidebooks, a set of workbooks provide a series of exercises and sample papers in which to practise the skills introduced in the guidebooks.

Entering Rockschool Examinations

It's now easier than ever to enter a Rockschool examination. Simply go to *www.rockschool.co.uk/enter-online* to book your exam online today.

Syllabus Content Overview

An overview of the syllabus content covered at this grade can be found at the back of this book. As this is a cumulative syllabus, you can download overviews for all grades from the Rockschool website at *www.rockschool.co.uk/theory* along with other theory syllabus related resources.

Exam Format

The exam has four sections. These are:

- **Music Notation** (20%)
  In this section, all questions relate to music notation.

- **Popular Music Harmony** (25%)
  In this section, all questions relate to music harmony.

- **Band Knowledge** (25%)
  This section is in two parts, with each part covering a range of instruments:
  – **Part 1:** Identification
  – **Part 2:** Notation and Techniques

- **Band Analysis** (30%)
  In this section, the questions will include the identification of music notation, harmony and the stylistic characteristics of drums, guitar, bass, keys and vocals in a multi-instrumental context.

Section 1 | Music Notation

SUMMARY	
SECTION *(Current section highlighted)*	**MARKS**
> **Music Notation**	**20 [20%]**
Popular Music Harmony	25 [25%]
Band Knowledge	25 [25%]
Band Analysis	30 [30%]

The *Music Notation* section of Rockschool Theory Examinations covers the following:

- 1.1   Pitch
- 1.2   Note length/rhythm
- 1.3   Dynamics, articulations and phrasing

You will be presented with a variety of exercises to hone your understanding and skills in these areas within the content specified for this grade.

Content Overview
An overview of the syllabus content covered at this grade can be found at the back of this book. As this is a cumulative syllabus, you can download overviews for all grades from the Rockschool website at *www.rockschool.co.uk*.

Section 1 | Music Notation

Rhythm | Double dotted notes

1. In the bar on the right, create a note of the same length as that on the left by joining several shorter notes with ties. Do not use dotted notes in your answer:

2. In the bar on the right, create a note of the same length as that on the left by joining several shorter notes with ties. Do not use dotted notes in your answer:

3. In the bar on the right, create a note of the same length as that on the left by joining several shorter notes with ties. Do not use dotted notes in your answer:

Rhythm | Less-common time signatures

1. Add barlines to the following musical example:

2. Add barlines to the following musical example:

3. Add barlines to the following musical example:

Rhythm | Rewriting with a new time signature

1. Rewrite the three bars of music from the top stave into four bars of music on the bottom stave in the new time signature:

2. Rewrite the four bars of music from the top stave into three bars of music on the bottom stave in the new time signature:

3. Rewrite the four bars of music from the top stave into six bars of music on the bottom stave in the new time signature:

Section 1 | Music Notation

Rhythm | Rewriting between compound and simple time

1. Rewrite the rhythm below into the compound time signature on the empty stave:

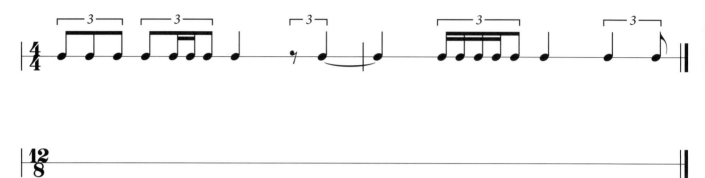

2. Rewrite the rhythm below into the simple time signature on the empty stave:

3. Rewrite the rhythm below into the simple time signature on the empty stave:

Pitch | Double accidentals

1. Circle two notes of the same pitch on each of the staves below:

2. Circle two notes of the same pitch on each of the staves below:

   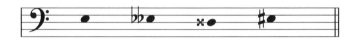

3. Circle two notes of the same pitch on each of the staves below:

Pitch | Writing enharmonic pitches

1. Add two enharmonically equivalent notes to those below. The result should be three notes of the same pitch on each stave, and each will be enharmonically spelled differently:

2. Add two enharmonically equivalent notes to those below. The result should be three notes of the same pitch on each stave, and each will be enharmonically spelled differently:

3. Add two enharmonically equivalent notes to those below. The result should be three notes of the same pitch on each stave, and each will be enharmonically spelled differently:

Section 1 | Music Notation

Pitch | Enharmonic transposition

1. Rewrite the music from the top stave into the empty stave below. The two keys are enharmonically identical, so the resulting music should sound the same:

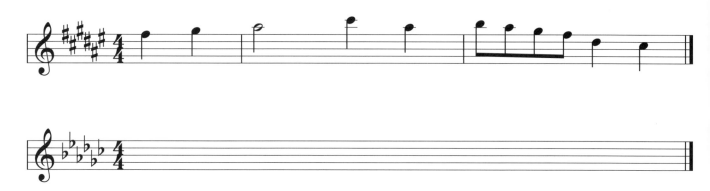

2. Rewrite the music from the top stave into the empty stave below. The two keys are enharmonically identical, so the resulting music should sound the same:

3. Rewrite the music from the top stave into the empty stave below, transposing from F♯ major into G♭ major and using accidentals rather than a key signature. The result should be enharmonically identical:

Section 2 | Popular Music Harmony

SUMMARY	
SECTION *(Current section highlighted)*	**MARKS**
Music Notation	20 [20%]
> **Popular Music Harmony**	**25 [25%]**
Band Knowledge	25 [25%]
Band Analysis	30 [30%]

The *Popular Music Harmony* section of Rockschool Theory Examinations covers the following:

- 2.1 Scales and related intervals
- 2.2 Chords

You will be presented with a variety of exercises to hone your understanding and skills in these areas within the content specified for this grade.

Content Overview

An overview of the syllabus content covered at this grade can be found at the back of this book. As this is a cumulative syllabus, you can download overviews for all grades from the Rockschool website at *www.rockschool.co.uk*.

Section 2 | Popular Music Harmony

Intervals | Interval identification

1. Identify each melodic interval by ticking one of the boxes below each example:

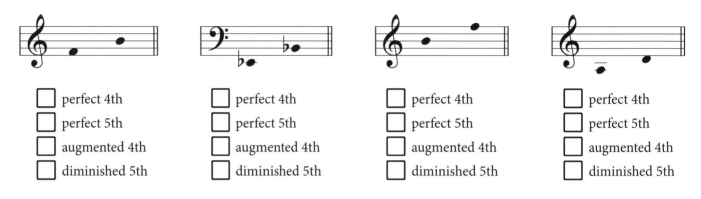

perfect 4th	perfect 4th	perfect 4th	perfect 4th
perfect 5th	perfect 5th	perfect 5th	perfect 5th
augmented 4th	augmented 4th	augmented 4th	augmented 4th
diminished 5th	diminished 5th	diminished 5th	diminished 5th

2. Identify each melodic interval by writing its name on the line below each stave:

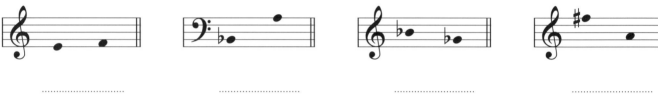

....

3. Identify each melodic interval by writing its name on the line below each stave:

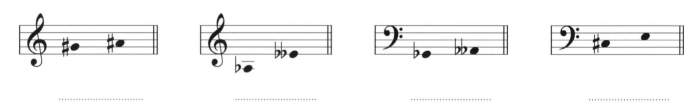

....

4. Add a note to each stave to create the requested harmonic interval:

major 6th above   octave above   minor 3rd above   perfect 4th below

5. Add a note to each stave to create the requested harmonic interval:

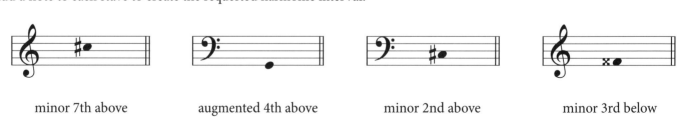

minor 7th above   augmented 4th above   minor 2nd above   minor 3rd below

Modes | Modal basics

1. C Ionian mode is known by another name. Write that name on the line below the stave:

C ionian mode

Your answer: ....

2. A Aeolian mode is known by another name. Write that name on the line below the stave:

A aeolian mode

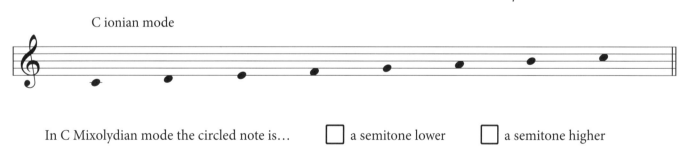

Your answer: ....

Modes | Modal transformation

3. Circle a note and tick one box to show how C Ionian mode can be transformed into C Mixolydian mode:

C ionian mode

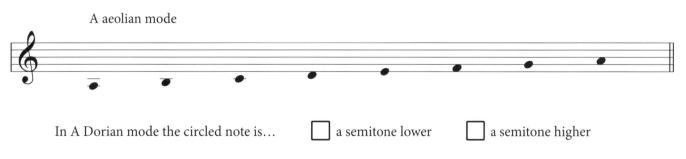

In C Mixolydian mode the circled note is… ☐ a semitone lower   ☐ a semitone higher

4. Circle a note and tick one box to show how A Aeolian mode can be transformed into A Dorian mode:

A aeolian mode

In A Dorian mode the circled note is… ☐ a semitone lower   ☐ a semitone higher

Section 2 | Popular Music Harmony

Modes | Modal differences

1. The G Ionian mode is show below – circle any notes that are different to the G Mixolydian mode:

G ionian mode

2. The G Ionian mode is show below – circle any notes that are different to the G Aeolian mode:

G ionian mode

3. The G Ionian mode is show below – circle any notes that are different to the G Dorian mode:

G ionian mode

Modes | Modal knowledge

1. Add the missing accidentals to the following mode:

E mixolydian mode

2. Add the missing accidentals to the following mode:

A dorian mode

3. Add the missing accidentals to the following mode:

B♭ aeolian mode

Modes | Writing out modes in notes

1. Using whole notes, write out a one-octave *ascending* D Mixolydian mode:

2. Using whole notes, write out a one-octave *ascending* E♭ Aeolian mode:

3. Using whole notes, write out a one-octave *ascending* F Dorian mode:

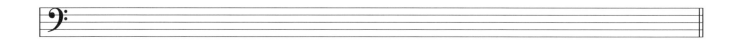

Modes | Writing out modes in note names

1. Write out the note names of the B♭ Mixolydian mode:

   Your answer: ....

2. Write out the note names of the F Aeolian mode:

   Your answer: ....

3. Write out the note names of the E♭ Dorian mode:

   Your answer: ....

Section 2 | Popular Music Harmony

Scales | Country scale

1. Rewrite the D major pentatonic scale from the upper stave onto the empty stave below, making any adjustments necessary to convert it to the D country scale:

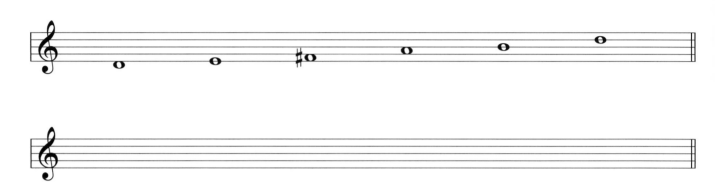

2. Rewrite the E♭ major pentatonic scale from the upper stave onto the empty stave below, making any adjustments necessary to convert it to the E♭ country scale:

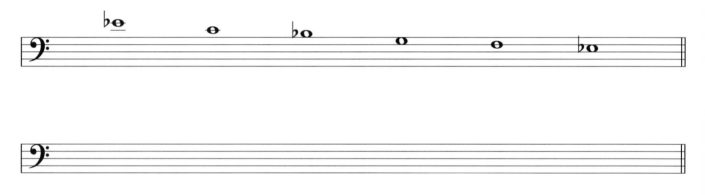

3. Rewrite the F♯ major pentatonic scale from the upper stave onto the empty stave below, making any adjustments necessary to convert it to the F♯ country scale:

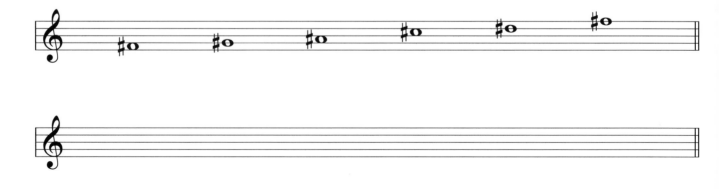

Scales | Scale recap

1. Using whole notes, write a one-octave *ascending* scale of each of requested scale. Use accidentals instead of a key signature:

E major

E natural minor

E harmonic minor

E major pentatonic

E minor pentatonic

E country

E blues

Section 2 | Popular Music Harmony

Chromaticism | Completing chromatic scales

1. Add the notes required to complete a one-octave chromatic scale:

2. Add the notes required to complete a one-octave chromatic scale:

3. Add the notes required to complete a one-octave chromatic scale:

Chromaticism | Gaps in chromatic scales

1. Add the missing notes in the following one-octave chromatic scale:

2. Add the missing notes in the following one-octave chromatic scale:

3. Add the missing notes in the following one-octave chromatic scale:

Chromaticism | **Writing out chromatic scales**

1. Using whole notes, write out a one-octave *descending* chromatic scale starting on F♯:

2. Using whole notes, write out a one-octave *ascending* chromatic scale starting on A♭:

3. Using whole notes, write out a one-octave *descending* chromatic scale starting on D♭:

Chromaticism | **Identifying chromatic fragments**

1. Put a circle around any short chromatic passages (there may be more than one), including those that change direction:

2. Put a circle around any short chromatic passages (there may be more than one), including those that change direction:

3. Put a circle around any short chromatic passages (there may be more than one), including those that change direction:

Transposition | Transposing in major 3rds and perfect 5ths

1. Transpose the passage on the left up a major 3rd to the empty stave on the right, using the appropriate key signature:

2. Transpose the passage on the left up a major 3rd to the empty stave on the right, using the appropriate key signature:

3. Transpose the passage on the left up a major 3rd to the empty stave on the right, using accidentals instead of a key signature:

4. Transpose the passage on the left up a perfect 5th to the empty stave on the right, using the appropriate key signature:

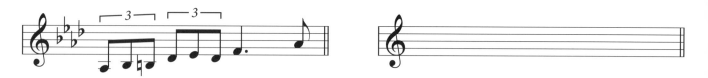

5. Transpose the passage on the left up a perfect 5th to the empty stave on the right, using the appropriate key signature:

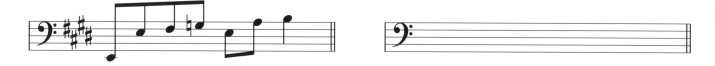

6. Transpose the passage on the left up a perfect 5th to the empty stave on the right, using accidentals instead of a key signature:

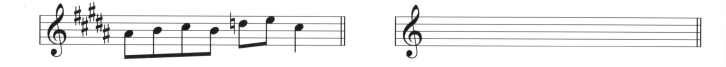

Transposition | Transposing chord charts

1. Transpose the following chord chart up a major 3rd. Write the new chart on the lower stave:

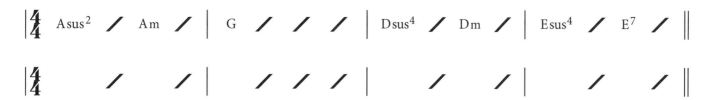

2. Transpose the following chord chart down a major 3rd. Write the new chart on the lower stave:

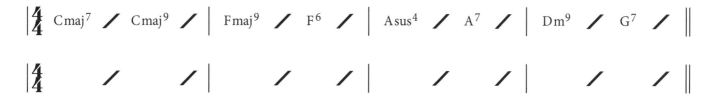

3. Transpose the following chord chart up a perfect 5th. Write the new chart on the lower stave:

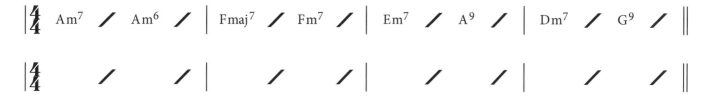

Chords | Chord inversions

1. Write out the following chords:

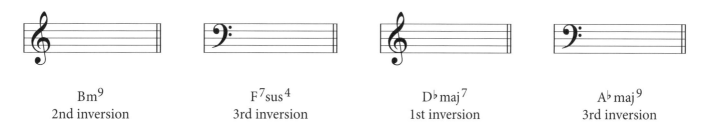

Bm^9
2nd inversion

F^{7}sus^4
3rd inversion

D$^\flat$maj^7
1st inversion

A$^\flat$maj^9
3rd inversion

2. Write out the following chords:

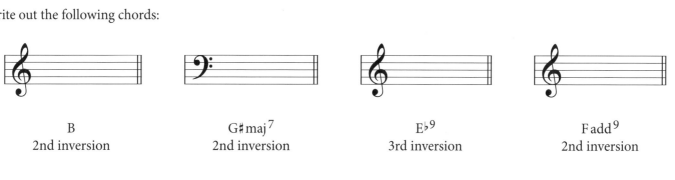

B
2nd inversion

G$\sharp$maj^7
2nd inversion

E$^\flat$^{9}
3rd inversion

Fadd^9
2nd inversion

Section 2 | Popular Music Harmony

Chords | Chord identification

1. Copy the chord names below to the appropriate chords:

C sus⁴   C⁷   C   C⁷sus⁴   C⁶   C m⁹   C⁹   C maj⁷

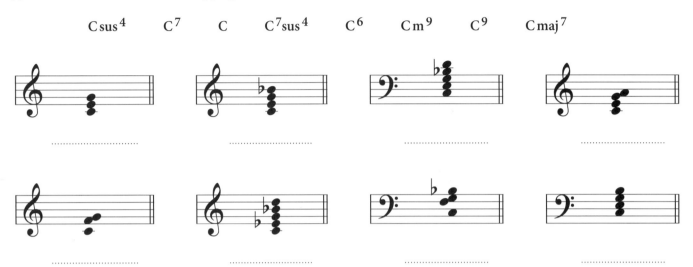

....

....

2. Identify the following chords by writing their names on the dotted line below the stave:

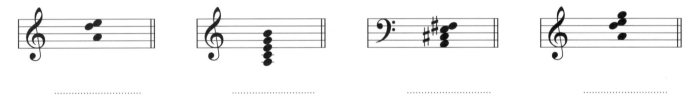

....

3. Identify the following chords by writing their names on the dotted line below the stave:

....

4. Identify the following chords by writing their names on the dotted line below the stave:

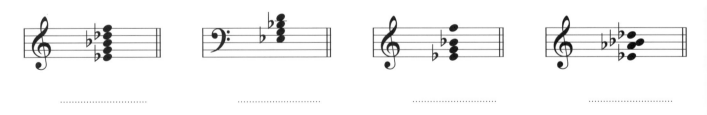

....

5. Identify the following chords by writing their names on the dotted line below the stave:

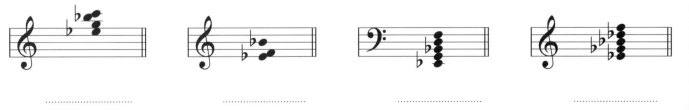

....

SECTION 3 | BAND KNOWLEDGE

SUMMARY	
SECTION *(Current section highlighted)*	**MARKS**
Music Notation	20 [20%]
Popular Music Harmony	25 [25%]
> **Band Knowledge**	**25 [25%]**
Band Analysis	30 [30%]

The *Band Knowledge* section of Rockschool Theory Examinations covers the following:

- 3.1 Identify instrument parts and function
- 3.2 Identify instrument-specific notation
- 3.3 Identify instrumental techniques

You will be presented with a variety of exercises to hone your understanding and skills in these areas within the content specified for this grade.

Content Overview

An overview of the syllabus content covered at this grade can be found at the back of this book. As this is a cumulative syllabus, you can download overviews for all grades from the Rockschool website at *www.rockschool.co.uk*.

Section 3 | Band Knowledge

Part 1 | Identification | Drums

The following five questions refer to the image on the right:

1. Name three different cymbals shown in the image:

   ....

2. Which cymbal has a clutch?

   ....

3. Which set of drums is not floor mounted?

   ....

4. On which instrument would you find a metal rattle strung under the bottom head?

   ....

5. Does the kit use a single or double bass-drum pedal?

   ....

- -

6. What are the advantages of a thicker drumstick? ....

   ....

7. What are the advantages of a thinner drumstick? ....

   ....

8. What are the advantages of a longer drumstick? ....

   ....

9. What are the advantages of a smaller tip? ....

   ....

Fill in the blanks:

10: A .... is a small, usually square socket wrench that fits over the ....

located at the edge of the .... These are turned clockwise to ....

the pitch and anti-clockwise to .... the pitch.

11: The hi-hat .... is used to secure the .... to the hi-hat

...., which moves up and down on the fixed .... cymbal when

operated by the ....

12: A typical kit has two or three toms. .... and .... toms are mounted

on or over the ...., with a .... tom set up on the floor with legs or

hung off a stand.

Section 3 | Band Knowledge

Part 1 | Identification | Guitar and Bass

1. Which type of pick has a clear, bright sound? *(Tick one box)* ☐ Thin ☐ Thick

2. Which type of pick has a warm, full sound? *(Tick one box)* ☐ Thin ☐ Thick

3. Give one advantage of using a thin pick: ....

   ....

4. Give one disadvantage of using a thin pick: ....

   ....

5. Give one advantage of using a thick pick: ....

   ....

6. Give one disadvantage of using a thick pick: ....

   ....

The following three questions refer to the image on the right:

7. What type of guitar is featured in the image?

   ....

8. What are the metal strips called?

   ....

9. What is the name of the part of the neck into which the metal strips are embedded?

   ....

----

10. Give four different ways in which an amp can change the sound of a guitar:

   i

   ....

   ....

   ii

   ....

   ....

   iii

   ....

   ....

   iv

   ....

   ....

11. Describe the process of sound being produced from the moment a string is picked to the moment the sound comes out of an amp. Include the following terms in your description:

   (1) *String*   (2) *Vibration*   (3) *Pickup*   (4) *Jack cable*   (5) *Amplifier*   (6) *Signal*

   Your answer: ....

   ....

   ....

   ....

   ....

   ....

   ....

   ....

   ....

   ....

Section 3 | Band Knowledge

Part 1 | Identification | Keys

The following three questions refer to the three images of pianos below:

Identify the different pianos from the images of their hammers, strings or other features: *(Tick one box per question)*

1. Which image shows a grand piano? ☐ A ☐ B ☐ C

2. Which image shows an upright piano? ☐ A ☐ B ☐ C

3. Which image shows an electronic keyboard? ☐ A ☐ B ☐ C

- -

4. Give three reasons why a grand piano tends to have a more rich and balanced tone than an upright piano:

    i ....

    ii ....

    iii ....

5. Give three advantages of an electronic keyboard over an acoustic piano:

    i ....

    ii ....

    iii ....

6. Give three advantages of an acoustic piano over an electronic keyboard:

    i ....

    ii ....

    iii ....

7. Which type of keyboard has the longest strings? *(Tick one box)*

    ☐ Grand Piano   ☐ Upright piano   ☐ Electronic keyboard

8. Which type of keyboard has a 'Middle C'? *(Tick one or more boxes)*

    ☐ Grand Piano   ☐ Upright piano   ☐ Electronic keyboard

9. Which type of keyboard has a power socket? *(Tick one or more boxes)*

    ☐ Grand Piano   ☐ Upright piano   ☐ Electronic keyboard

10. Which type of keyboard has a vertical hammer-action? *(Tick one or more boxes)*

    ☐ Grand Piano   ☐ Upright piano   ☐ Electronic keyboard

11. Which type of keyboard has both black and white keys? *(Tick one or more boxes)*

    ☐ Grand Piano   ☐ Upright piano   ☐ Electronic keyboard

12. Which type of keyboard uses sampled sounds? *(Tick one or more boxes)*

    ☐ Grand Piano   ☐ Upright piano   ☐ Electronic keyboard

13. Which type of keyboard has vertical strings? *(Tick one or more boxes)*

    ☐ Grand Piano   ☐ Upright piano   ☐ Electronic keyboard

14. Which type of keyboard can play more than one key at a time? *(Tick one or more boxes)*

    ☐ Grand Piano   ☐ Upright piano   ☐ Electronic keyboard

15. Which type of keyboard has a volume-control button? *(Tick one or more boxes)*

    ☐ Grand Piano   ☐ Upright piano   ☐ Electronic keyboard

16. Which type of keyboard has horizontal strings? *(Tick one or more boxes)*

    ☐ Grand Piano   ☐ Upright piano   ☐ Electronic keyboard

Section 3 | Band Knowledge

Part 1 | Identification | Vocals

1. Which type of microphone is most suited to live performances? *(Tick one box)*

    ☐ Dynamic microphone   ☐ Condenser microphone

    Give a reason for your answer: ....

    ....

2. Which type of microphone is most suited to studio use? *(Tick one box)*

    ☐ Dynamic microphone   ☐ Condenser microphone

    Give a reason for your answer: ....

    ....

3. Which microphone is good for capturing loud instruments? *(Tick one box)*

    ☐ Dynamic microphone   ☐ Condenser microphone

4. Which microphone captures a smaller range of frequencies? *(Tick one box)*

    ☐ Dynamic microphone   ☐ Condenser microphone

----

5. Describe the function of the larynx in singing:

    Your answer: ....

    ....

6. Describe the function of the nasal cavity in singing:

    Your answer: ....

    ....

7. Describe the function of the diaphragm in singing:

    Your answer: ....

    ....

8. A PA amplifies the sound captured by a microphone. What is PA short for? *(Tick one box)*

   ☐ Personal Amplification   ☐ Power Amplifier

   ☐ Public Address   ☐ Portable Amp

- -

True or false:

9. A PA system can amplify only one sound at a time:

   ☐ True   ☐ False

10. A PA can amplify other sounds including non-vocal instruments:

    ☐ True   ☐ False

11. A PA can amplify more than one vocalist but doesn't accept input of non-vocal instruments:

    ☐ True   ☐ False

12. Each input is given its own channel for individual adjustments:

    ☐ True   ☐ False

13. A PA system has four basic controls: volume, bass, middle and treble:

    ☐ True   ☐ False

14. PA systems are primarily used in recording studios:

    ☐ True   ☐ False

Section 3 | Band Knowledge

Part 1 | Notation & Techniques | Saxophone

The following questions require you to identify parts of the saxophone as depicted in the labelled images on the right. Each part is only referenced once:

1. Which part is labelled 'A'? *(Tick one box)*

   ☐ Body   ☐ Mouthpiece

   ☐ Neck   ☐ Keys

2. Which part is labelled 'B'? *(Tick one box)*

   ☐ Body   ☐ Mouthpiece

   ☐ Neck   ☐ Keys

3. Which part is labelled 'C'? *(Tick one box)*

   ☐ Body   ☐ Mouthpiece

   ☐ Neck   ☐ Keys

4. Which part is labelled 'D'? *(Tick one box)*

   ☐ Body   ☐ Mouthpiece

   ☐ Neck   ☐ Keys

True or false:

5. The flared end of the saxophone is called the bell: ☐ True   ☐ False

6. The U-shaped bend at the bottom is called the bowl: ☐ True   ☐ False

7. The straight main section of the body is called the tube: ☐ True   ☐ False

----

8. The player-operated 'buttons' that cover and uncover the tone holes, making an airtight seal with their leather pads when closed, are called: *(Tick one box)*

   ☐ Caps   ☐ Keys   ☐ Lids

Band Analysis Score 1

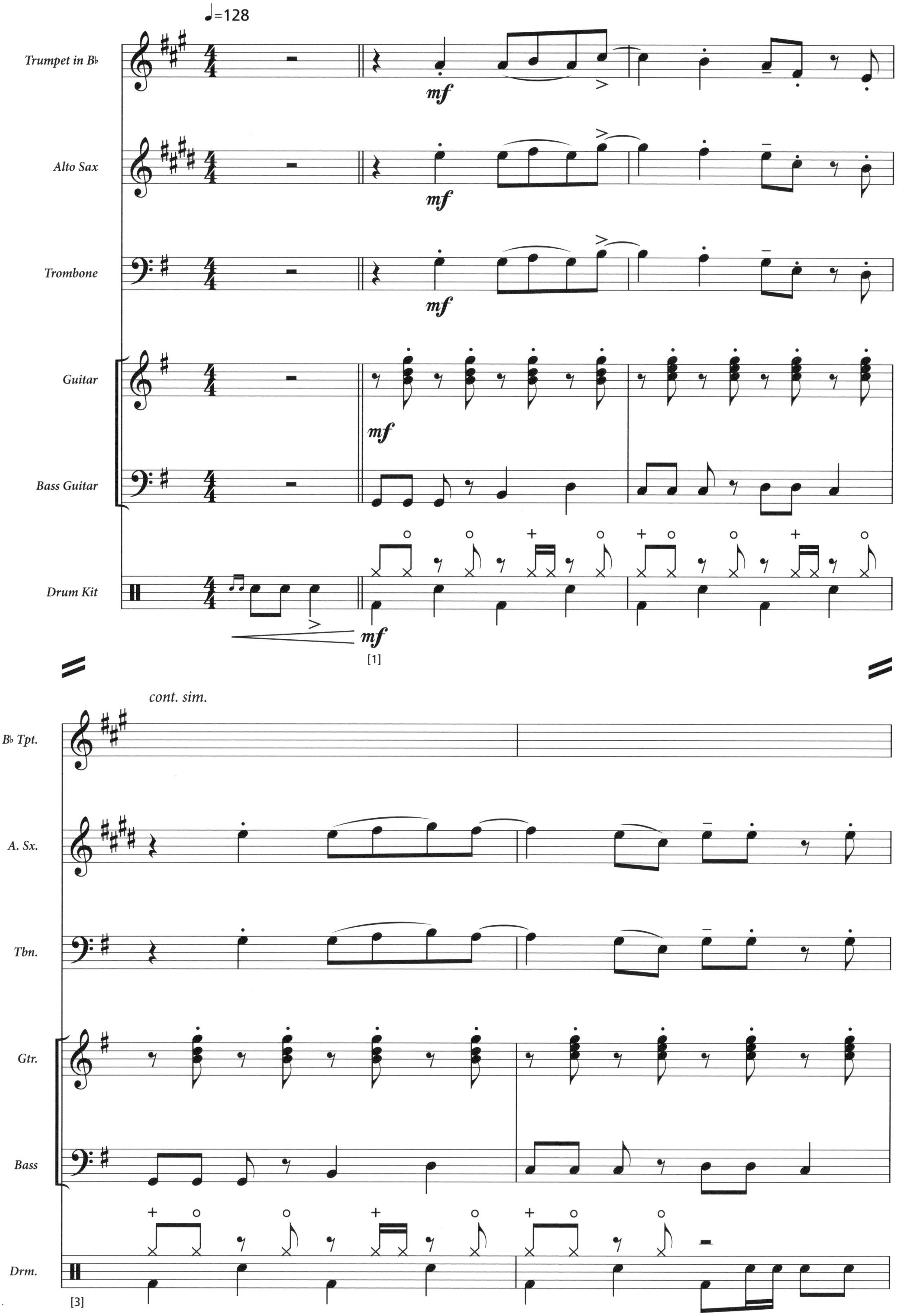

Band Analysis Score 2

Vox. (m.5): sun fell in-to the night____ and the

Vox. (m.7): moon is not so bright,____ but I

♩=64
Vocals
Piano
pp
Guitar
mp
Bass Guitar
mp
Drum Kit

Vox.
Try as I might to get through on the phone to you, the
mf
Pno.
mf
Gtr.
mf
Bass
mf
Drm.
mf
[3]

mes - sage that I get___ is you're en - gaged,_____ I don't know what___ to do.___

cont. sim.

develop

[5]

I'm get - ting friend - ly with the op - er - a - tor___

[7]

may - be I'll date her in - stead of you.____

need   no   oth - er   light____   but   you.____

develop

Part 1 | Identification | Trumpet

The following four questions refer to the labelled image on the right:

1. Identify the different parts of the trumpet:

   A: ....

   B: ....

   C: ....

   D: ....

True or false:

2. The overall tuning of the trumpet is adjusted using the main bell: ☐ True ☐ False

3. The shape of the mouthpiece directly influences the tone: ☐ True ☐ False

4. There are four valves on a trumpet: ☐ True ☐ False

5. The sound emanates from the trumpet bell: ☐ True ☐ False

Fill in the blanks:

6. The overall tuning of the trumpet is adjusted using the main .... at the end of the leadpipe.

   To raise the .... it is pushed in to shorten the air column and pulled out to lengthen it

   which in turn .... the pitch.

7. The valves of the trumpet are used to route the .... through the valve

   ...., increasing the length of the air column and .... the pitch

   of the note played.

Section 3 | Band Knowledge

Part 1 | Identification | Trombone

The following question refers to the labelled image on the right:

1. Identify the different main parts of the trombone:

   A: ....

   B: ....

   C: ....

   D: ....

Fill in the blanks:

2: The raw tone of the trombone is created by the .... of the player making an air-

   tight seal with the .... and being forcibly 'buzzed' to vibrate the column of air within

   the instrument.

3: The hand slide slides in and out of the .... section to change the length of the tubing and

   the column of air within, thus modulating the .... of the note heard when the mouthpiece is

   blown correctly.

4: Made of brass, the .... section is the curved tube that extends from the slide receiver to

   the flared end of the trombone. In the playing position, this section rests on the .... of

   the trombonist.

5: The tuning slide is a section of tubing forming the .... between the neck and the bell that

   can be slid in and out, altering the pipe length of the trombone and changing its overall ....

   as a result.

Part 2 | Notation & Techniques | Drums

The following three questions refer to the two-bar extract of drum notation below:

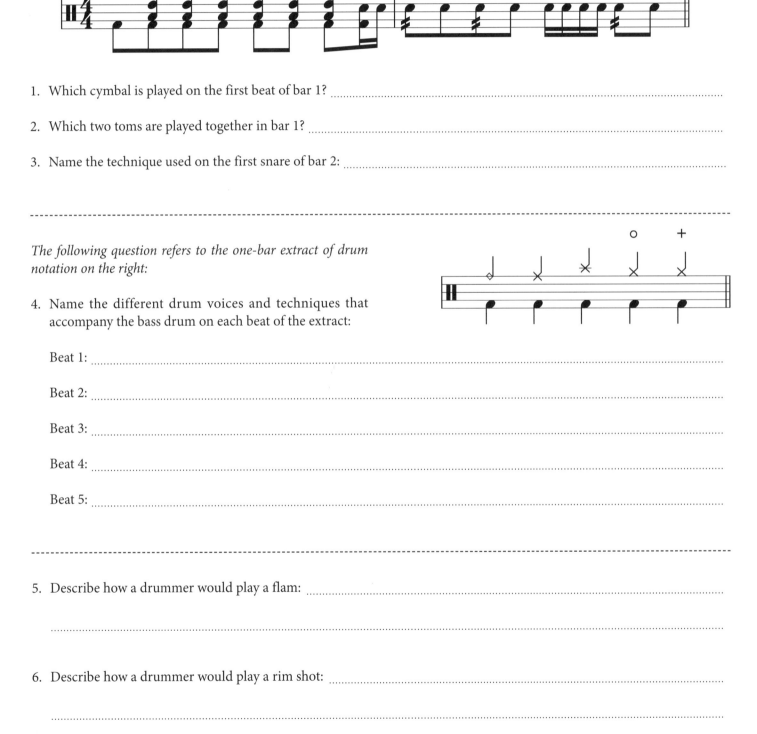

1. Which cymbal is played on the first beat of bar 1? ....

2. Which two toms are played together in bar 1? ....

3. Name the technique used on the first snare of bar 2: ....

The following question refers to the one-bar extract of drum notation on the right:

4. Name the different drum voices and techniques that accompany the bass drum on each beat of the extract:

   Beat 1: ....

   Beat 2: ....

   Beat 3: ....

   Beat 4: ....

   Beat 5: ....

----

5. Describe how a drummer would play a flam: ....

   ....

6. Describe how a drummer would play a rim shot: ....

   ....

7. Describe how a ghost snare would be played: ....

   ....

Section 3 | Band Knowledge

Part 2 | Notation & Techniques | Guitar and Bass

The following three questions refer to the one-bar extract of guitar notation below:

1. Name and describe the technique used to play the first three notes of the bar: ....

   ....

   ....

   ....

   ....

2. Name and describe the technique used to play the fourth note of the bar: ....

   ....

   ....

   ....

   ....

3. Name and describe the technique used to play the final two notes of the bar: ....

   ....

   ....

   ....

   ....

The following three questions refer to the one-bar extract of guitar notation below:

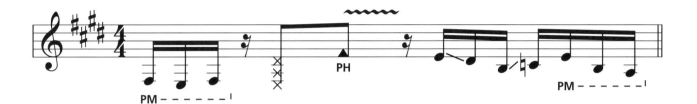

1. Explain what the PM stands for, and how a guitarist would play the first three notes of the extract: ....

....

....

....

....

2. Explain how the guitarist would play the chord on the second beat of the bar (notated with X noteheads): ....

....

....

....

....

3. Explain what the PH stands for, and how a guitarist would play it: ....

....

....

....

....

Part 2 | Notation & Techniques | Keyboards

The following five questions refer to the two-bar extract of piano music below:

1. Identify the vertical wavy line on beat 2 of bar 1 in the left hand, and describe how this is played: ....

   ....

   ....

2. Identify the articulation placed over the first chord of bar 1 in the left hand, and describe how this is played: ....

   ....

   ....

3. In which bar and on which beat is the trill played? ....

   ....

   ....

4. How would a pianist play a trill? ....

   ....

   ....

5. Which hand plays staccato notes, and how are they played? ....

   ....

   ....

The following three tasks require you to add notation to the two-bar extract of piano music below:

1. Above the first note of the first bar in the right hand, add a tenuto symbol.

2. Between the second and third notes of the second bar, add a glissando indication.

3. In the first bar, add staccatos to all of the 16th notes in the right hand.

Section 3 | Band Knowledge

Part 2 | Notation & Techniques | Vocals

The following three questions refer to the two-bar extract of vocal music below:

1. Name the symbol, technique and effect on performance of the curved line at the end of bar 1: ....

   ....

   ....

   ....

   ....

   ....

2. Describe how the final word of bar 2 is sung: ....

   ....

   ....

   ....

   ....

3. Name the three diagonal line symbols used in the piece, and describe how they each affect the performance: ....

   ....

   ....

   ....

   ....

The following three questions refer to the labelled vocal ranges on the right:

Each bar shows the three areas of the soprano vocal range. Identify which bar most closely represents these:

4. Mix voice: *(Tick one box)*   ☐ A   ☐ B   ☐ C

5. Head voice: *(Tick one box)*   ☐ A   ☐ B   ☐ C

6. Chest voice: *(Tick one box)*   ☐ A   ☐ B   ☐ C

Ⓐ   Ⓑ   Ⓒ

- -

7. Describe what you understand by the term 'head voice':

....

....

....

....

....

8. Describe what you understand by the term 'mix voice':

....

....

....

....

....

9. Describe what you understand by the term 'chest voice':

....

....

....

....

Section 3 | Band Knowledge

Part 2 | Notation & Techniques | Trumpet

1. Identify the correct statement: *(Tick one box)*

   ☐ The trumpet is a B♭ transposing instrument.

   ☐ The trumpet is an E♭ transposing instrument.

   ☐ The trumpet is an F transposing instrument.

True or false:

2. Music notation written for the trumpet usually uses the bass clef : ☐ True ☐ False

---

The following question refers to the four bars of music shown below:

Notated music Ⓐ Ⓑ Ⓒ

3. If the notes in the bar on the left (labelled 'Notated music') were played on the trumpet, which of the three bars on the right (labelled 'A', 'B' and 'C') represents the actual pitches that would be heard? *(Tick one box)*

   ☐ A   ☐ B   ☐ C

The following question refers to the four labelled instrument ranges shown below:

Ⓐ Ⓑ Ⓒ Ⓓ

4. Which of the four pitch ranges above (labelled 'A' to 'D') best represents the range of a trumpet? Base your answer on the written range, rather than the actual pitch sounded: *(Tick one box)*

   ☐ A   ☐ B   ☐ C   ☐ D

Part 2 | Notation & Techniques | Trombone

All the following questions regarding the trombone are referring to the most common trombone – the tenor trombone.

1. Identify the correct statement: *(Tick one box)*

    ☐ The trombone is not a transposing instrument.

    ☐ The trombone is an F transposing instrument.

    ☐ The trombone is an E♭ transposing instrument.

True or false:

2. The tenor trombone has a wider pitch range than both the trumpet and the alto saxophone: ☐ True   ☐ False

----

The following question refers to the four bars of music shown below:

Notated music   (A)   (B)   (C)

3. If the notes in the bar on the left (labelled 'Notated music') were played on the trombone, which of the three bars on the right (labelled 'A', 'B' and 'C') represents the actual pitches that would be heard? *(Tick one box)*

    ☐ A   ☐ B   ☐ C

The following question refers to the four labelled instrument ranges shown below:

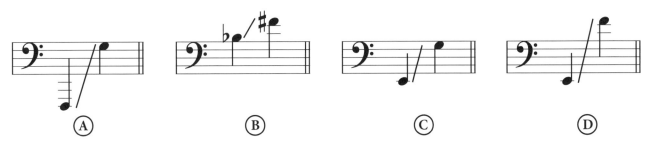

(A)   (B)   (C)   (D)

4. Ignoring the pedal range and extended range, which of the four pitch ranges above (labelled 'A' to 'D') best represents the range of a trombone? *(Tick one box)*

    ☐ A   ☐ B   ☐ C   ☐ D

Section 3 | Band Knowledge

Part 2 | Notation & Techniques | Alto Saxophone

1. Identify the correct statement: *(Tick one box)*

☐ The alto saxophone is not a transposing instrument

☐ The alto saxophone is a B♭ transposing instrument

☐ The alto saxophone is an E♭ transposing instrument

- -

True or false:

2. A transposing instrument is a musical instrument whose sound is different to the notated pitch:

☐ True ☐ False

3. If a pianist and an alto saxophonist are playing the same song together, the parts that they are reading from will be written in different keys:

☐ True ☐ False

- -

The following question refers to the four bars of music shown below:

Notated music   Ⓐ   Ⓑ   Ⓒ

4. If the notes in the bar on the left (labelled 'Notated music') were played on the alto saxophone, which of the three bars on the right (labelled 'A', 'B' and 'C') represents the actual pitches that would be heard? *(Tick one box)*

☐ A ☐ B ☐ C

- -

The following question refers to the four labelled instrument ranges shown below:

Ⓐ   Ⓑ   Ⓒ   Ⓓ

5. Which of the four pitch ranges above (labelled 'A' to 'D') best represents the range of an alto saxophone? Base your answer on the written range, rather than the actual pitch heard: *(Tick one box)*

☐ A ☐ B ☐ C ☐ D

BAND ANALYSIS

SUMMARY	
SECTION *(Current section highlighted)*	**MARKS**
Music Notation	20 [20%]
Popular Music Harmony	25 [25%]
Band Knowledge	25 [25%]
> **Band Analysis**	**30 [30%]**

The *Band Analysis* section of Rockschool Theory Examinations covers the following:

- 4.1   Identify general music features
- 4.2   Accurately complete a score
- 4.3   Identify instrument-specific techniques and stylistic traits
- 5.1   Identify harmonic structure and appropriate scales for improvisation

You will be presented with a variety of exercises to hone your understanding and skills in these areas within the content specified for this grade.

Content Overview
An overview of the syllabus content covered at this grade can be found at the back of this book. As this is a cumulative syllabus, you can download overviews for all grades from the Rockschool website at *www.rockschool.co.uk*.

Section 4 | Band Analysis

Band Analysis | Score 1

The following five questions relate to the 12-bar pull-out score titled "Band Analysis Score 1". Note that there are blank areas which will be filled in as part of the tasks below:

Part 1 | Improvisation

1. Complete the trumpet part by writing out a suitable cont. sim. part in bars 3–6.
2. Complete the drum part by writing out a suitable development section in bars 5–8, incorporating a fill into the part.

Part 2 | Style and Content

3. Write a brief analysis of bars 7–10 of the guitar part, naming and describing any features that have identifiable stylistic traits. You may include references to any musical devices, melodic/harmonic/rhythmic content, and instrument-specific techniques that you see in the part:

   Your answer:
   ....
   ....
   ....
   ....
   ....

4. Briefly discuss the harmonic content and form of the score:

   Your answer:
   ....
   ....
   ....
   ....
   ....

5. Locate, name and describe two other features in the score that have significant stylistic traits:

   Your answer:
   ....
   ....
   ....
   ....

Band Analysis | Score 2

The following five questions relate to the 12-bar pull-out score titled "Band Analysis Score 2". Note that there are blank areas which will be filled in as part of the tasks below:

Part 1 | Improvisation

1. Complete the piano part by writing out a suitable cont. sim. part in bars 5–8.
2. Complete the bass-guitar part by writing out a suitable development section in bars 5–8, incorporating a fill into the part.

Part 2 | Style and Content

3. Write a brief analysis of bars 1–4 of the piano part, naming and describing any features that have identifiable stylistic traits. You may include references to any musical devices, melodic/harmonic/rhythmic content, and instrument-specific techniques that you see in the part:

   Your answer:

   ....
   ....
   ....
   ....
   ....

4. Briefly discuss the harmonic content and form of the score:

   Your answer:

   ....
   ....
   ....
   ....
   ....

5. Locate, name and describe two other features in the score that have significant stylistic traits:

   Your answer:

   ....
   ....
   ....
   ....
   ....

SAMPLE PAPER

The following pages contain examples of the types of questions you will find in a Grade 6 exam paper. They give an indication of the content, format, layout and level at this grade.

You will see the exam paper has been split into the same four sections that have been presented earlier in this workbook:

- Music Notation
- Popular Music Harmony
- Band Knowledge
- Band Analysis

Content Overview

- **Marking:**
    - The exam is marked out of a total of 100, and the total available marks for each section are clearly stated at the start of each section. There is also a blank markbox where your total examination score can be noted.
    - The total marks available for each question are displayed on the right, and include a space for your teacher to mark your answers.

- **General advice:**
    - If a question requires a written answer, don't feel compelled to use every line. Answering the question correctly is much more important than using all the available space.
    - Aim to answer all the questions set. If you get stuck on one particular question, move on and come back to it later.

- **Neatness:**
    - Your answers should be neat, accurate and legible as marks cannot be given if your response is ambiguous.
    - Avoid unnecessary corrections by thinking your responses through before committing them to paper.
    - Use a pencil that is sharp enough to write precisely, but soft enough to rub out and make corrections.
    - To avoid confusion, tick boxes (checkboxes) should be marked with a clear tick symbol rather than a cross. Please note that some answers require more than one box to be ticked, so read the questions carefully.

Please visit *www.rockschool.co.uk* for detailed information on all Rockschool examinations, including syllabus guides, marking schemes and examination entry information.

Grade 6 | Sample Paper

Section 1 | Music Notation

Mark:

Q 1.01 | Rewrite the three bars of music from the top stave into four bars of music on the bottom stave in the new time signature:

5

Q 1.02 | Rewrite the rhythm below into the compound time signature on the empty stave:

5

Q 1.03 | Circle two notes of the same pitch on each of the staves below:

4

Q 1.04 | In the bar on the right, create a note of the same length as the bar on the left by joining several shorter notes with ties. Use as few notes as possible and do not used dotted notes in your answer:

Q 1.05 | Rewrite the music in the top stave into the empty stave below, maintaining the same pitch, and using as few accidentals as possible:

4

Grade 6 | Sample Paper

Section 2 | Popular Music Harmony

Total marks for this section: 25

Mark:

Q 2.01 | Identify the following two harmonic intervals and write your answers on the lines below each example: [2]

....

Q 2.02 | Add a note to the right of each of the notes to create the requested melodic interval: [3]

major 7th below   augmented 4th below   major 6th above

Q 2.03 | Complete the chromatic scale by adding the missing notes indicated by a question mark: [3]

Q 2.04 | Add the missing accidentals to the mode below: [2]

D aeolian mode

Q 2.05 | Write out the following chords: `4`

E major	G♯ maj⁷	E♭ add9	D maj⁹
2nd inversion	2nd inversion	1st inversion	3rd inversion

Q 2.06 | Name this chord: `1`

C   E   G   B♭   D

Your answer:

Q 2.07 | The following chord sequence is in the key of G major. Add Roman numeral notation on the line provided below the stave: `5`

Q 2.08 | Copy the following four-bar chord sequence in the key of C minor onto the lower stave, transposing it into the new key of E minor: `5`

Grade 6 | Sample Paper

Total marks for this section: 25

Mark:

Q 3.01 | Which part of the drum kit has a metal rattle strung under the bottom head?

[1]

Your answer:

Q 3.02 | Give one advantage of using a longer drumstick:

[1]

Your answer:

Q 3.03 | Give one advantage of using a thin pick:

[1]

Your answer:

Q 3.04 | Give two different ways in which an amp can change the sound of a guitar:

[2]

A.

B.

Q 3.05 | Which type of keyboard instrument has a vertical hammer action?

[1]

Your answer:

Q 3.06 | Give one advantage of a grand piano over an upright piano in a recording or performance situation:

> 1

Your answer:

....

....

Q 3.07 | Which type of microphone is best suited to live performance?

> 1

Your answer:

....

Q 3.08 | Which type of microphone is best suited to studio use?

> 1

Your answer:

....

Q 3.09 | What is the flared end of a saxophone called?

> 1

Your answer:

....

Q 3.10 | How many valves are there on a trumpet?

> 1

Your answer:

....

The following two questions refer to the labelled image below:

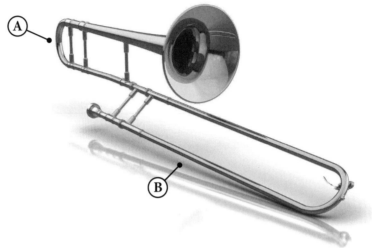

Q 3.11 | Name the part of the trombone labelled 'A': [1]

Your answer: ....

Q 3.12 | Name the part of the trombone labelled 'B': [1]

Your answer: ....

Section 3 | Band Knowledge | Part 2 – Notation & Techniques

Q 3.13 | Describe how a drummer would play a rim shot:

[ ] 1

Your answer:

....

....

....

- -

Q 3.14 | Describe how a drummer would play a flam:

[ ] 1

Your answer:

....

....

....

- -

The following two questions relate to the one-bar extract of guitar notation below:

Q 3.15 | Explain what the PH means in beat 2?

[ ] 1

Your answer:

....

....

....

Q 3.16 | Explain how a guitarist would play the final note of the bar:

[ ] 1

Your answer:

....

....

....

- -

Grade 6 | Sample Paper

The following two questions relate to the two-bar extract of piano music below:

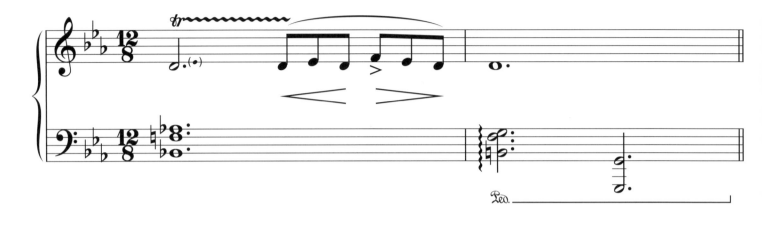

Q 3.17 | Name the technique used in the right-hand part in bar 1, beats 1 & 2, and explain what is involved in playing this correctly:

`1`

Your answer:

....

....

....

....

Q 3.18 | In bar 2 beat 1, how would the left-hand chord be played?

`1`

Your answer:

....

....

....

....

The following two questions relate to the two-bar extract of vocal notation below:

lead   you   on   a   mer - ry   dance   and   find ___   won - der - land.

Q 3.19 | Name the technique indicated by the wavy line above the last note of the piece:

`1`

Your answer: ....

Q 3.20 | Would this extract of music be in the head voice, mix voice or chest voice range of a soprano? *(Tick one box)*

`1`

☐ Head voice   ☐ Mix voice   ☐ Chest voice

Q 3.21 | Which is the correct pitch range for a trumpet? *(Tick one box)*

`1`

☐ A

☐ B

☐ C

☐ D

Q 3.22 | The bar on the left is the notated music. Which of the three bars labelled 'A', 'B' and 'C' would be the correct pitch that the trombone would sound?

Notated version (A) (B) (C)

Tick one box: ☐ A ☐ B ☐ C

Q 3.23 | Identify the correct statement by ticking one box: *(Tick one box)*

☐ The alto saxophone is a B♭ transposing instrument.

☐ The alto saxophone is an E♭ transposing instrument.

☐ The alto saxophone is an F transposing instrument.

☐ The alto saxophone is not a transposing instrument.

Q 3.24 | Which is the correct pitch range for an alto saxophone? *(Tick one box)*

☐ A

☐ B

☐ C

☐ D

Section 4 | Band Analysis

The following five questions relate to the 12-bar pull-out score titled "Band Analysis Score 3". Note that there are blank areas which will be filled in as part of the tasks below:

Q 4.01 | Complete the piano part by writing out a suitable cont. sim. part in bars 5–7, and a chordal part to support the guitar and bass guitar in bar 8.

[10]

Q 4.02 | Complete the drum part by writing out a suitable development section in bars 5–8.

[10]

Q 4.03 | Write a brief analysis of bars 1–4 of the guitar part, naming and describing any features that have identifiable stylistic traits. You may include references to any musical devices, melodic/harmonic/rhythmic content, and instrument-specific techniques that you see in the part:

[3]

Your answer:

....

....

....

....

Q 4.04 | Briefly discuss the harmonic content and form of the score:

[3]

Your answer:

....

....

....

....

Q 4.05 | Locate, name and describe two other features in the score that have significant stylistic traits:

4

Your answer:

....

....

....

....

....

Important: This table represents content that is new at this grade. The content of Rockschool Theory Examinations is cumulative, so Grades 1 to 8 include all content from previous grades in the syllabus. A full version of this table is available online at *www.rockschool.co.uk*, and includes details of content at every grade.

Section	Content	Details
1. Music Notation (20%)	1.1: Pitch	accidentals: double flats, double sharps
	1.2: Note length/rhythm	note lengths: double dotted notes
		16th-note triplet
		time signatures: $\frac{2}{2}\frac{3}{2}\frac{4}{2}$
2. Popular Music Harmony (25%)	2.1: Scales and related intervals	major scales: F♯, G♭
		natural and harmonic minor scales: D♯m, E♭m
		other scales: chromatic, country (all keys)
		modes: Ionian, Aeolian, Dorian, Mixolydian
		melodic and harmonic intervals: augmented 4th, diminished 5th
		inverted intervals
	2.2 Chords	major chords: F♯, G♭
		major arpeggios: F♯, G♭
		minor chords: D♯m, E♭m
		minor arpeggios: D♯m, E♭m
		chord inversions: 3rd inversions
		extended chords: add chords, 6, m^6, 6/9, $m^{6/9}$, sus^2, sus^4, maj^9, m^9, dom^9 chords
		transposition: 3rds, 5ths
3. Band Knowledge (25%)	3.1: Identify instrument parts and function	drums: stick thickness, length, tip
		guitar and bass guitar: thin & thick picks
		keys: upright, grand, electric keyboard
		vocals: condensor, dynamic microphones
		alto saxophone: body, keys, mouthpiece, neck
		trumpet: bell, mouthpiece, tuning slide, valves
		tenor trombone: mouthpiece, hand slide, tuning slide, bell
	3.2: Identify instrument-specific notation	drum notation: buzz roll
		guitar and bass-guitar notation: tapping
		keys notation: spread, rolling chords
		vocal notation: head voice, mix voice, chest voice
		alto saxophone notation: transposition, range
		trumpet notation: transposition, range
		tenor trombone: transposition, range
	3.3: Identify instrument-specific techniques	as listed above in 3.2
4. Band Analysis (30%)	4.1: Identify general music features listed	identify and show understanding of the applied musical elements listed within the first three sections (above) within the context of a score
		instrument range: drum kit, guitar, bass guitar, keyboard, vocals, alto saxophone, trumpet, trombone
		number of parts: 5–8 parts
		piece length: 12 bars
	4.2: Accurately complete a score	be able to construct a 2–4 bar cont. sim./ develop/ad lib. part for any of the instruments listed within the 5–8 part score, to include a fill
	4.3: Identify instrument-specific techniques and stylistic traits	as listed within part 3 (above)
		identify stylistic devices used within the score (pop, blues, rock, metal, funk, reggae, soul, jazz, country)
	5.1: Identify harmonic structure and appropriate scales for improvisation	identify appropriate scale for improvising over a chord sequence within the score: scales and modes as listed within part 2 (above)
		analyse harmonic structure

rockschool®

ENTER ONLINE

Ready to take your Rockschool Theory Exam?

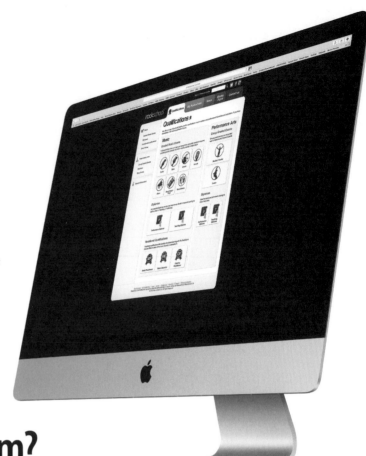

Now it's easier than ever...

1 GO TO WWW.ROCKSCHOOL.CO.UK/ENTER-ONLINE

2 CREATE AN ACCOUNT

3 SELECT YOUR EXAM CENTRE AND DATE

4 CHOOSE YOUR GRADE

... and you're ready to go.

Book your exam today – go to **www.rockschool.co.uk/enter-online**, or email **info@rockschool.co.uk** for more information.